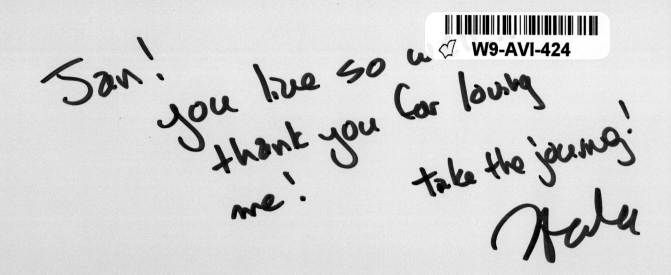

Jan! you live so ... thank you for loving me! take the journey! *[signature]*

A Reluctant Missionary

An Everyday Mama Shoved by God into a Sierra Leone Adventure

By Heather Curlee Novak

This book is dedicated to
John, Portia and Libby Novak
and to
Family in all forms
and all places.

My first trip outside the United States was in 2019 on a mission from my church, First United Methodist Church of Valparaiso, Indiana, to Sierra Leone West Africa. Up to that time, I had no interest in world missions or global travel. I felt there was already great need in the local community around me. I gave to local charities and sponsored children globally through World Vision and Compassion International.

Then I learned about the Taiama Enterprise Academy (TEA) located in the Taiama village in Sierra Leone, West Africa. My church was sending a mission to Sierra Leone through Operation Classroom and I was invited to go. The mission was to facilitate a pen pal relationship between the young people of Sierra Leone and the youth in my local community. I had several reasons not to go, including the fact that I was recovering from Bell's Palsy. I was also raising two young daughters who needed their mother.

Wherever I turned it seemed all my objections and concerns were being met with a Divine "YES". There was strong support and encouragement from my family members and friends. People suggested solid solutions to counter all my worries. I felt strongly that God meant for this to happen and I do not argue with "ol Padnah". I gave in.

After four months of preparation I had my passport, the gear and supplies that would be needed. I was intellectually prepared for the mission. I was not prepared emotionally for Sierra Leone. I am a blogger and share regular radio commentary on NPR Michiana Chronicles. I was looking forward to writing and had several journals to capture my experience. Sierra Leone was so different from the world I knew! As I waded into my days, the journals remained empty and I felt I had lost my voice.

I found myself unable to communicate beyond a few moments captured here and there in haiku. My father had taught me haiku and I occasionally jotted thoughts and memories into the 5-7-5 syllable, three line Japanese form poems. In Sierra Leone, I found it simpler to restrict what I felt in my heart to this pattern. I composed 54 Haiku in Sierra Leone.

My new friends, some mentioned in the verses to follow, make me care about Africa. I care about this scrappy STEM school for entrepreneurs amidst primitive villages and unpaved roads. I hope these photos and haiku will also touch your heart and mind as you turn each page. I hope you explore our world, too.

Proceeds from this book will go to support the TEA School in Sierra Leone through Operation Classroom.

MUSK

Sierra Leone
has a fragrance of it's own
Rich with unwashed life.

Salone #1

FAVORITES

Tiny Adamah
Shimmies with her smile
I laugh and dance too!

-Salone #2

CAMERA

Selfie! Selfie! Yes!
Humble homes but still cell phones
everyone gets in.

-Salone #3

WHITE PEOPLE

Pumwee! The Pumwee!
They pull my hair and touch me
the minority

-Salone #4

STEAMY

Sweat trickles down my...
I need ICE! Powder! Water!
Fans are heavenly.

-Salone # 5

MYSTERY

Salone food is good
a little bit of spicy
maybe cassava?

-Salone # 6

BIGGEST SMILES

Poverty a joy?
to live simply with your love
dirt not withstanding.

-Salone #7

SIERRA LEONE AMERICANA

S'leone cheeseburger
french fries were the next day tho?
warm food, warm people.

-Salone # 8

BOY SCOUTS

Scouting is the same:
Uniformed honor and pride,
International!

-Salone #9

CAGED

Little hands through bars
privilege separates me
sadly I watch them.

-Salone #10

HANDS OUT

If I give to them
they will drown me in their need
how much is enough?

-*Salone #11*

CULTURAL DEMONSTRATION

The devil dancer
shaking for evil or good?
dancing for money.

-Salone #12

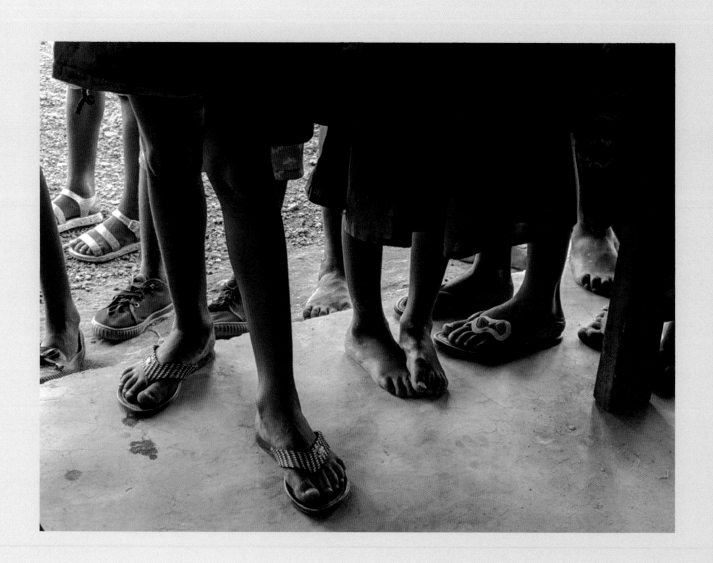

NOTHING ELSE TO DO

54 children
my brain cannot handle it
one man, 15 wives...

-Salone #13

PORCH LIFE

Real community
comfort outside rain or shine
front porch visiting.

-Salone #14

FUTILITY

my morning routine
looking at deodrant
laughing, put it on.

Salone #15

FUTILITY

My morning routine
looking at deodorant
laughing, put it on.

-Salone #15

ON REPEAT

No snooze button here
repetitive rooster's crow
broken alarm clock.

-Salone #16

COLD WATER

Refreshment is mine
sweaty night, sweaty days too
trickling shower.

-Salone #17

VANITY

Every bathroom here
stripped down, never a mirror
no one wants to see.

-Salone #18

BANANA BREAK

Pregnant girl selling
one dollar feeds the workers
we buy everything.

-Salone #19

IMPROVISED UMBRELLA

Rain begins to fall
chickens under wheelbarrow
resourceful creatures.

-Salone #20

CHEAP THRILL

Motorcycle ride
I forgot to pay the man
looking for Amar?

-Salone #21

SENEGAL SIDEWALK STORY

Walking together
staying way too close to me
hand in my pocket?

-Salone #22

PLAY

Hanging out, watching
Morrison and Mustafa
teach us hoop rolling!

-Salone #23

MISSING MY DAUGHTERS

Video magic
Libby connects from Valpo
"Dancing with hats on!"

-Salone #24

BLOCK/BRICKS

No Menards here
carry loads of sand to mix
cement blocks are made

-Salone #25

CUTTHROAT

Greatest Uno game
shaking with helpless laughter
everybody wins.

-Salone #26

IBRAHIM SAVES

"I see you people
moving" (Pumwee do not move?)
"I came to help you!"

-Salone #27

TOEING THE LINE

We joke together
humorous witty jabs and
double entendres

-Salone #28

PICK UP ARTIST

Little baby goat
I do not squeeze too hard
But unhappy mama!

-*Salone #29*

CULTURAL EXCHANGE

Gifts us bananas
He asks us for a bible
Salone John Brewer

-Salone #30

BIENVENUE

Our Star Therapy!
Empty gas station,
cookie communion.

-Salone #31

EWWW!

I screamed like a girl
bigger than a man's finger?
Surprise centipede!

-Salone #32

PLEASE?

Communication:
Her body was an eye roll...
Removed from her work.

-Salone #33

GOT CHANGE?

The girl student shows
a five inch paper penny
scraped together change.

-Salone #34

ABUNDANT FOWL

Most often charbroiled
Oh! Chicken, chicken, chicken!
I long for salad?

-Salone #35

THIS IS AFRICA

We aren't teaching
culture clash on achievement
we are just learning.

-Salone #36

WEATHER REPORT

Hot Hot Hot Hot Hot
Sweaty sweat sweat sweat sweaty
Hot Hot Hot Hot Hot.

-Salone #37

NEED

My time for prayer
nothing I could ask for now
Equilibrium?

-Salone #38

WATER BOTTLE

All the thirsty ones
Lazarus everywhere here
I'm the only one.

-Salone # 39

PROGRESS

Jesus lived like this
You tell us to help us cope
Backwards time machine.

-Salone #40

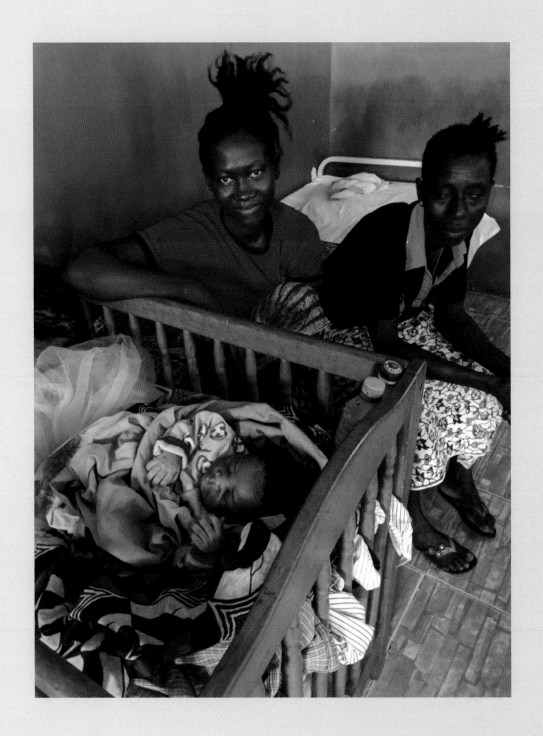

SHARE!

Hungry people stare
we all dish out what we have
the leftover food.

-Salone #41

WORLDLY

Bo supermarket
weird Kitkats and other things
Reese's are the same.

-Salone #42

NOT MONKEY

Ninety-six percent
closest relative
Chimpanzee reserve.

-Salone #43

HOLD ON!

Breathtaking dirt roads
Toyota can scale it well
rollercoaster fun?

-Salone #44

MAYHEM

Roll your window up
flash money, they try our doors
desperate sellers...

-Salone #45

R&R

The whitest beaches
Fresh saltwater on my lips
River Number Two

-Salone #46

TOP SALES

Fumbling Leons
beauty for haggled sale here
mobile discount store

-Salone #47

MARKET

Hello, Friend! Look here!
I give you nice price on that.
(Repeat fifty times.)

-Salone #48

HOPE

Two smiling faces:
Sulaimon and Emerson
Take care of those boys!

-Salone #49

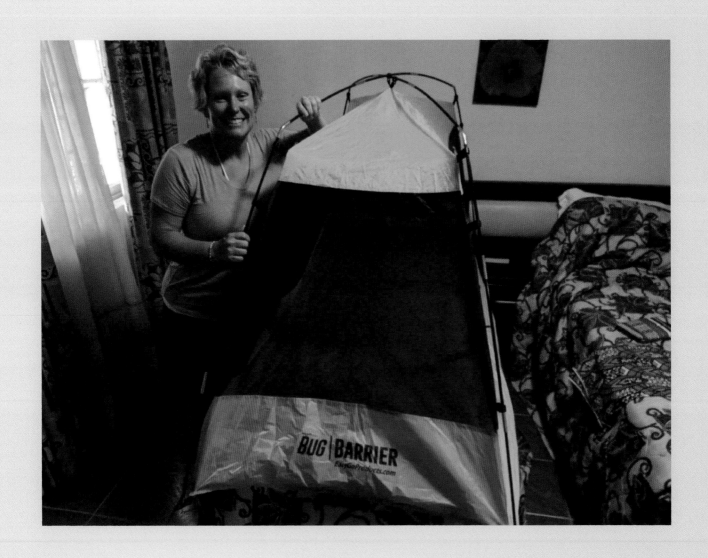

JEALOUS MUCH?

Thank you for the laughs
your ridiculous bug tent
Radiant Greta!

-Salone #50

TRUTH IN ADVERTISING?

City of Freetown
"The New York of Africa!"
That might be a reach...

-Salone #51

CHILDREN

They play on trash beach
tourists diverted away
You "Allee! Allee!"

-Salone #52

HOMEWARD

It's twenty-four hours
Cars, boats, trains, airplanes
Traveling the world.

-Salone #53

MISSION

Lord, thank you for this.
Experience teaches me,
help me REMEMBER!

-Salone #54

ACKNOWLEDGEMENTS

This book is one of the many ways God has blown my mind with this trip to a tiny village in Africa. I am constantly humbled, amused and grateful for the ways He chooses to move in my life. Thank you, Ol Padnah!

Without the loving encouragement and investment from my Uncle Frank and Aunt Ruth Lutes, the book you hold in your hands would still be pictures on a Google drive and a leather bound journal full of chicken scratch haiku.

I want to thank Mike Strayer, Bonnie Albert, Margie Miller, Mike Yohe, Mike Wuebbling, Sandy Coolman and Kathi Thompson from Valpo FUMC International Missions Team for encouraging me to go on this trip.

Big thanks to the trip team; Monty Barker, Greta Carroll, Warren Buckler, my Pastor Kevin Miller and Pastor Bob Coolman as the trip coordinator.

Love to the Sierra Leone Team including Mr. Joseph Pormai, Director of Secondary Education in UM Schools, Mr. Jonathan Lamboi AKA "Air Force One" and Mr. Imbrahim Sensesie AKA "Air Force Two" and Mr. Duramany Massavoi, Managing Director of the TEA..

Thanks to my Haiku writing Dad, Jim Curlee and my Bonus Parents John and Monte Novak for all the love, support and childcare!

Hugs and highlighters to Lucas Ecklund Baker and Kasey Fickett for enduring my printed color coordinated schedule and child wrangling. Double thanks to Lucas for financial support in memory of his brother Jake W. Baker. Thanks to Jean DeWinter, Amy Ahiga, Janet Peterson and Amy Knauff for advice and supplies.

Gratitude to my prayer warriors Jenny "Joy" Arndt, the members and staff of Valpo FUMC, the Mafia Dames of United Methodist Women and all the fierce mamas of Valpo Modern Moms.

A final thank you to my beloved mate John Monte Novak and our daughters Portia Katherine and Elizabeth "Libby" Novak. You three gracefully let me go on this life changing trip to Africa. John, I was humbled by your response when I first told you about the possibility of this crazy trip. You said, "Well, you'll need a passport." and that was it. The three of you continue to offer me more adventure and joy than I could imagine. I hope to take you with me to the TEA someday soon.

RESOURCES

Operation Classroom

Operation Classroom helps young people in Liberia and Sierra Leone grow into educated and productive adults who can make a positive impact on our world and end the cycle of poverty. The Taiama Enterprise Academy, AKA "The T.E.A." is Sierra Leone's first Entrepreneurial STEM School. To find out more go to www.operationclassroom.org or find them on Social Media as "Operation Classroom".

Heather Curlee Novak

Heather is a national speaker, writer and consultant helping people with the zeitgeist of modern life. She lives with her Personal Prince Charming John and two young daughters. Listen to her NPR radio commentary with Michiana Chronicles, read her blog or invite Heather to speak. She will engage and inspire your group to work and live simply better lives. Find her on social media or at www.HeatherNovakSPEAKER.com